Mel Bay Presents

Folk Songs for Schools & Camps

By Jerry Silverman

Cover illustration by Greg Ragland.

*This book is available as a book only or as a book/compact disc configuration.

1 2 3 4 5 6 7 8 9 0

© 1991 BY MEL BAY PUBLICATIONS, INC., PACIFIC, MO 63069.
ALL RIGHTS RESERVED. INTERNATIONAL COPYRIGHT SECURED. B.M.I. MADE AND PRINTED IN U.S.A.
No part of this publication may be reproduced in whole or in part, or stored in a retrieval system, or transmitted in any form
or by any means, electronic, mechanical, photocopy, recording, or otherwise, without written permission of the publisher.

Visit us on the Web at www.melbay.com — E-mail us at email@melbay.com

Contents

Peace Like A River

Joyful, lively tempo   Spiritual

1. I've got peace like a riv - er, I've got peace like a riv - er, I've got

peace like a riv - er in my soul; I've got peace like a riv - er, I've got

peace like a riv - er, I've got peace like a riv - er in my soul.

I've got joy like a fountain, etc. . .   I've got love like on ocean, etc. . .

America

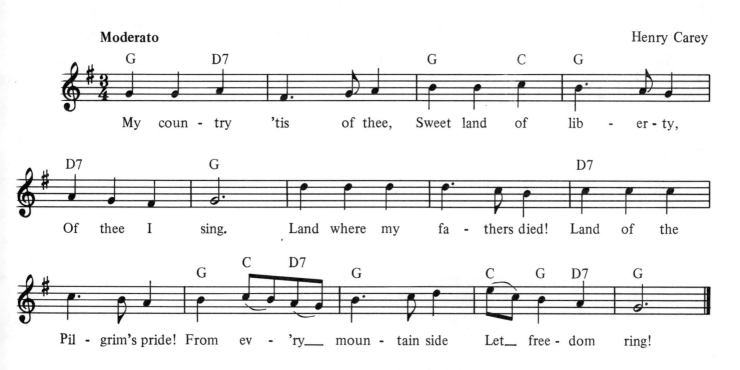

Moderato   Henry Carey

My coun - try 'tis of thee, Sweet land of lib - er - ty,

Of thee I sing. Land where my fa - thers died! Land of the

Pil - grim's pride! From ev - 'ry__ moun - tain side Let__ free - dom ring!

My Native country, Thee,
Land of the Noble free,
Thy name I love;
I love Thy rocks and rills,
Thy woods and templed hills
My heart with rapture thrills
Like that above.

America The Beautiful

By Katherine Lee Bates

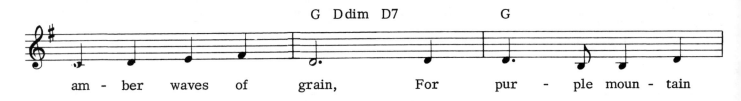

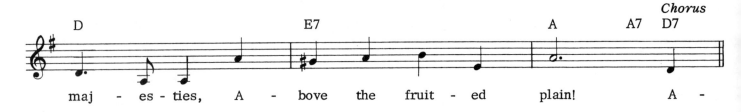

O beautiful for patriot dream
That sees beyond the years;
Thine alabaster cities gleam
Undimmed by human tears.

America! America!
God shed His grace on thee,
And crown thy good with brotherhood
From sea to shining sea.

Star Spangled Banner

Our National Anthem

The Keeper

Old English

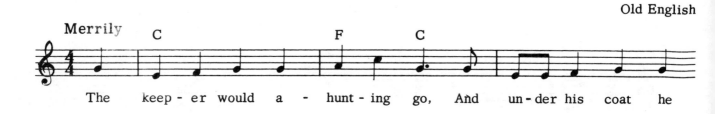

The keep-er would a-hunt-ing go, And un-der his coat he

car-ried a bow, All for to shoot at a mer-rie lit-tle doe, A-

mong the leaves so__ green, O. *Chorus* Jack-ie boy! Mas-ter! Sing ye well? Ve-ry well.

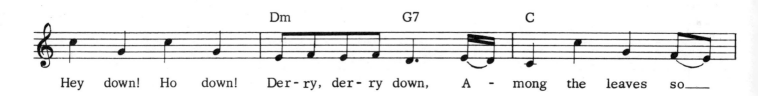

Hey down! Ho down! Der-ry, der-ry down, A-mong the leaves so__

green, O. To my hey down, down! To my ho down, down!

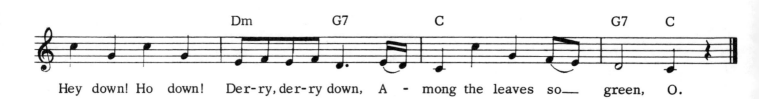

Hey down! Ho down! Der-ry, der-ry down, A-mong the leaves so__ green, O.

The first doe he shot at he missed;
The second doe he trimmed he kissed;
The third doe went where nobody wist
Among the leaves so green, O.
Chorus

The fourth doe she did cross the plain;
The keeper fetched her back again;
Where she is now she may remain
Among the leaves so green, O.
Chorus

The fifth doe she did cross the brook;
The keeper fetched her back with his crook;
Where she is now you must go and look
Among the leaves so green, O.
Chorus

The sixth doe she ran over the plain;
But he with his hounds did turn her again,
And it's there he did hunt in a merry, merry vein
Among the leaves so green, O.
Chorus

6

Bold Fisherman

There was a bold fish-er-man who sailed out from Pim-be-co To
slew the wild cod-fish and the bold mack-er-el. When he ar-rived off
Pim-be-co the storm-y winds did wild-ly blow. His lit-tle boat went
wib-ble, wob-ble, and o-ver-board sprang he. *(but he sang)*

Chorus:

Twink-i, doo-dle, dum, twink-i, doo-dle, dum, 'Twas the
high-ly in-ter-est-ing song he sung. "Twink-i doo-dle, dum, twink-i,
doo-dle, dum" sang the bold fish-er-man.

He wriggled and scriggled in the water,
   so briny - O
He yellowed and bellowed for help but
   in vain.
Then downward he did gently glide
To the bottom of the silvery tide;
But previously to this he cried
"Fare thee well, Mar-i-Jane!" *Chorus*

His ghost walked at midnight to the
   bedside of his Mar-i-Jane.
He told her how dead he was; said she,
   "I'll go mad."
"Since my lovey is so dead," said she,
"All joy on earth has fled for me;
I never more will happy be."
And she went staring mad. *Chorus*

'Round The Bay of Mexico

West Indian Folk Song

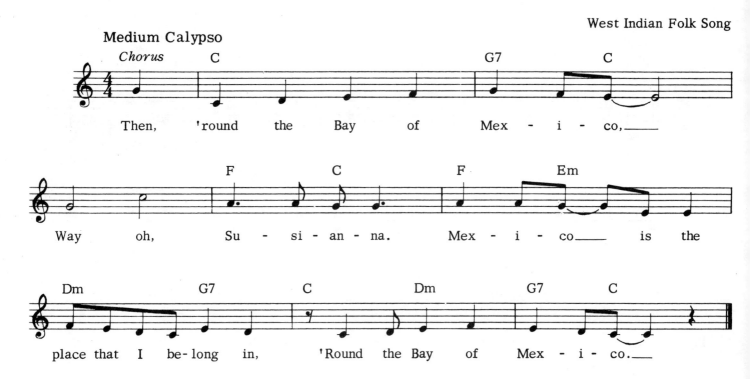

Medium Calypso

Chorus

Then, 'round the Bay of Mex - i - co,____

Way oh, Su - si - an - na. Mex - i - co____ is the

place that I be- long in, 'Round the Bay of Mex - i - co.____

When I was a young man in my prime,
 Way oh, Susianna!
I'd love those pretty girls two at a time,
 'Round the Bay of Mexico.
Chorus

The reason those girls they love me so,
 Way oh, Susianna!
Because I don't tell everything that I know,
 'Round the Bay of Mexico.
Chorus

Them Nassau girls ain't got no combs,
 Way oh, Susianna!
They comb their hair with whipper-back bones,
 'Round the Bay of Mexico.
Chorus

He's Got The Whole World In His Hands

Spiritual

He's got the whole world ___ in His hands, ___ He's got the

whole world ___ in His hands, ___ He's got the whole world ___

in His hands, ___ He's got the whole world in His hands. ___

He's got the wind and the rain in His hands,
He's got the sun and the moon in His hands,
He's got the wind and the rain in His hands,
He's got the whole world in His hands.

He's got you and me, brother, in His hands,
He's got you and me, brother, in His hands,
He's got you and me, brother, in His hands,
He's got the whole world in His hands.

He's got the little bitty baby in His hands,
He's got the little bitty baby in His hands,
He's got the little bitty baby in His hands,
He's got the whole world in His hands.

He's got everybody in His hands,
He's got everybody in His hands,
He's got everybody in His hands,
He's got the whole world in His hands.

Repeat Verse One

My Bonny Lies Over The Ocean

American Folk Song

Oh, blow, ye winds, over the ocean,
And blow, ye winds, over the sea.
Oh, blow, ye winds, over the ocean,
And bring back my Bonny to me.
Chorus

Last night as I lay on my pillow,
Last night as I lay on my bed,
Last night as I lay on my pillow,
I dreamed that my Bonny was dead.
Chorus

The winds have blown over the ocean,
The winds have blown over the sea,
The winds have blown over the ocean,
And brought back my Bonny to me.
Chorus

Lonesome Valley

Gospel Song

You mother's got to walk that lonesome valley,
She's got to walk it by herself.
Ain't nobody else can walk it for her,
She's got to walk that lonesome valley by herself.

Your father's got to walk that lonesome valley,
He's got to walk it by himself.
Ain't nobody else can walk it for him,
He's got to walk that lonesome valley by himself.

Your brother's got to walk that lonesome valley,
He's got to walk it by himself.
Ain't nobody else can walk it for him,
He's got to walk that lonesome valley by himself.

If you cannot preach like Peter,
If you cannot pray like Paul,
You can tell the love of Jesus,
You can say He died for all.

Swing Low, Sweet Chariot

Spiritual

Swing Low, Sweet Char - i - ot,— Comin' for to car - ry me home.

Swing Low, Sweet Char - i - ot,— Comin' for to car - ry me home.

Looked o - ver Jor - dan, What did I see?— Comin' for to carry me home? A

band of an - gels comin' af - ter me,— Comin' for to car - ry me home!

Shenandoah

O Shen-an-doah,— I long to hear you, A - way,— you roll-ing

riv - er.— Oh Shen-an-doah— I long to hear you, A -

way, — we're bound a - way, 'Cross the wide Mis - sou - ri.

The white man loved the Indian maiden. . .   O, Shenandoah, I love your daughter. . .
With notions his canoe was laden. . .   I'll take her 'cross the rolling water. . .

O, Shenandoah, I'm bound to leave you . . .
O, Shenandoah, I'll not deceive you . . .

Land Of The Silver Birch

Canadian Indian

Land of the sil - ver birch home of the bea - ver, And where the

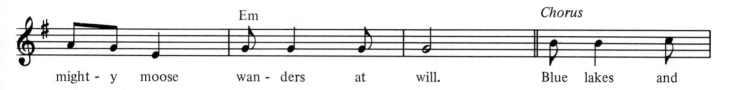

might - y moose wan - ders at will. Blue lakes and

rock - y shores, I will re - turn once more, Boom - did-dy-um - bum,_

___ bum - bum. Boom - did - dy - um - bum,_____ bum - bum.

High on a rocky ledge I'll build my wigwam,
Close by the water's edge silent and still. *Chorus*

Down in the forest glade deep in the lowlands,
My heart cries out for thee, Hills of the North. *Chorus*

Bury Me Not On The Lone Prairie

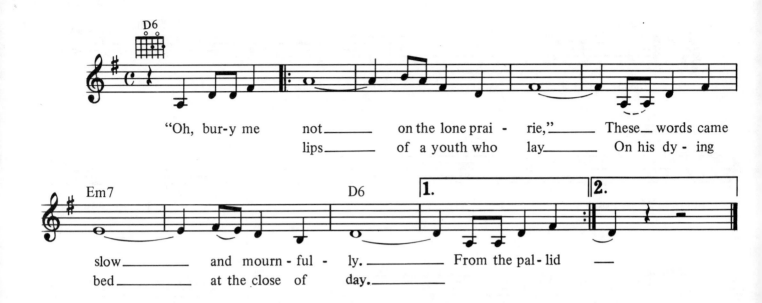

"Oh, bur-y me not_____ on the lone prai - rie,"_____ These__ words came
lips_____ of a youth who lay_____ On his dy - ing

slow_____ and mourn - ful - ly. _____ From the pal - lid —
bed_____ at the close of day._____

"Oh, bury me not on the lone prairie,
Where the wild coyotes will howl o'er me,
In a narrow grave just six by three.
Oh, bury me not on the lone prairie."

"It matters not, I've oft been told,
Where the body lies when the heart grows cold.
Yet grant, oh grant this wish to me:
Oh, bury me not on the lone prairie."

"I've always wished to be laid when I died
In the little churchyard on the green hillside.
By my father's grave there let mine be,
And bury me not on the lone prairie."

"Oh, bury me not"—and his voice failed there,
But we took no heed of his dying praper.
In a narrow grave just six by three
We buried him there on the lone prairie.

And the cowboys now as they roam the plain,
For they marked the spot where his bones were lain,
Fling a handful of roses o'er his grave
With a prayer to Him who his soul will save.

Crawdad

Southern Folk Song

Moderately fast

You get a line and I'll get a pole,___ Hon - ey.___

___ You get a line and I'll get a pole,___

Babe.___ You get a line and

I'll get a pole, And we'll go fish-in' by the craw - dad hole,___

Hon - ey,___ sug - ar ba - by mine.___

You get a line and I'll get a pole, Honey,
You get a line and I'll get a pole, Babe,
You get a line and I'll get a pole,
We'll go down to the crawdad hole,
Honey, sugar baby mine.

Yonder comes a man with a pack on his back...
Totin' all the crawdads he can pack...

A-settin' on the ice 'til my feet got cold...
A-watchin' that crawdad dig his hole...

Crawdad, crawdad, you'd better dig deep...
For I'm a-goin' to ramble in my sleep...

A-settin' on the ice 'til my feet got hot...
A-watchin' that crawdad rack and trot...

Crawdad, crawdad, you'd better go to hole...
If I don't catch you, damn my soul...

Whatcha gonna do when the lake runs dry?...
Sit on the bank and watch the crawdads die...

Blow The Man Down

English Sea Shanty

Rollicking

Chorus

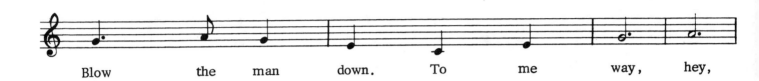

Oh, blow the man down, bul - lies,

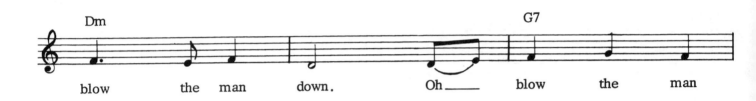

Blow the man down. To me way, hey,

blow the man down. Oh ___ blow the man

down, bul - lies, Blow him a - way,

Give me some time to blow the man down.

As I was a-walking down Paradise Street,
  To me way, aye, blow the man down,
A pretty young damsel I chanced for to meet,
  Give me some time to blow the man down.
Chorus

She was round in the counter and bluff in the bow,
  To me way, aye, blow the man down,
So I took in all sail and cried, "Way enough now!"
  Give me some time to blow the man down.
Chorus

I hailed her in English, she answered me clear,
  To me way, aye, blow the man down,
"I'm from the *Black Arrow* bound to the *Shakespeare*,"
  Give me some time to blow the man down.
Chorus

So I tailed her my flipper and took her in tow,
  To me way, aye, blow the man down,
And yardarm to yardarm away we did go,
  Give me some time to blow the man down.
Chorus

And as we were going she said unto me,
  To me way, aye, blow the man down,
"There's a spanking full-rigger just ready for sea."
  Give me some time to blow the man down.
Chorus

That spanking full-rigger for New York was bound,
  To me way, aye, blow the man down,
She was very well manned and very well found,
  Give me some time to blow the man down.
Chorus

But as soon as that packet was clear of the bar,
  To me way, aye, blow the man down,
The mate knocked me down with the end of a spar,
  Give me some time to blow the man down.
Chorus

And as soon as that packet was out on the sea,
  To me way, aye, blow the man down,
'Twas dev'lish hard treatment of every degree,
  Give me some time to blow the man down.
Chorus

So I give you fair warning before we belay,
  To me way, aye, blow the man down,
Don't never take heed of what pretty girls say,
  Give me some time to blow the man down.
Chorus

Clementine

19th Century American Folk Song

In a cav - ern, in a can - yon, Ex - ca -

vat - ing for a mine, Dwelt a min - er, for - ty

nin - er, And his daugh - ter, Clem - en - tine.

Chorus: Oh my darling, oh my darling, oh my darling Clementine,
       You are lost and gone forever, dreadful sorry, Clementine.

Light she was, and like a fairy, and her shoes were number nine,
Herring boxes without topses, sandals were for Clementine.
Chorus

Drove she ducklings to the water every morning just at nine,
Hit her foot against a splinter, fell into the foaming brine.
Chorus

Ruby lips above the water, blowing bubbles soft and fine,
Alas for me! I was no swimmer, so I lost my Clementine.
Chorus

Froggie Went A-Courtin'

Old English Folk Song

He rode up to Miss Mousie's door,
  A-hum, a-hum,
He rode up to Miss Mousie's door,
Where he had often been before.
  A-hum, a-hum.

He said, "Miss Mouse, are you within?"
  A-hum, a-hum.
He said, "Miss Mouse, are you within?"
"Just lift the latch and please come in."
  A-hum, a-hum.

He took Miss Mousie on his knee,
  A-hum, a-hum.
He took Miss Mousie on his knee,
And said, "Miss Mouse, will you marry me?"
  A-hum, a-hum.

"Without my uncle Rat's consent,"
  A-hum, a-hum.
"Without my uncle Rat's consent,
I would not marry the President."
  A-hum, a-hum.

Now uncle Rat, when he came home,
  A-hum, a-hum.
Now, uncle Rat, when he came home,
Said, "Who's been here since I've been gone?"
  A-hum, a-hum.

"A very fine gentleman has been here,"
  A-hum, a-hum.
"A very fine gentleman has been here,
Who wishes me to be his dear."
  A-hum, a-hum.

Then uncle Rat laughed and shook his sides,
  A-hum, a-hum.
Then uncle Rat laughed and shook his sides,
To think his niece would be a bride.
  A-hum, a-hum.

So, uncle Rat, he went to town,
  A-hum, a-hum.
Uncle Rat, he went to town
To buy his niece a wedding gown.
  A-hum, a-hum.

Where will the wedding breakfast be?
  A-hum, a-hum.
Where will the wedding breakfast be?
Away down yonder in the hollow tree.
  A-hum, a-hum.

What will the wedding breakfast be?
  A-hum, a-hum.
What will the wedding breakfast be?
Two green beans and a black-eyed pea.
  A-hum, a-hum.

The first to come was the bumblebee,
A-hum, a-hum.
The first to come was the bumblebee,
He danced a jig with Miss Mousie.
A-hum, a-hum.

The next to come was Mister Drake,
A-hum, a-hum.
The next to come was Mister Drake,
He ate up all of the wedding cake.
A-hum, a-hum.

They all went sailing on the lake,
A-hum, a-hum.
They all went sailing on the lake,
And they all got swallowed by a big black snake.
A-hum, a-hum.

So, that's the end of one, two, three,
A-hum, a-hum.
That's the end of one, two, three,
The Rat, the Frog and Miss Mousie.
A-hum, a-hum.

There's bread and cheese upon the shelf,
A-hum, a-hum.
There's bread and cheese upon the shelf,
If you want any more just sing it yourself.
A-hum, a-hum.

Aunt Rhody

Children's Folk Song

The one she's been savin' (*3 times*)
To make a feather bed.

She died in the millpond (*3 times*)
A-standin' on her head.

The old gander's mournin' (*3 times*)
Because his wife is dead.

The goslin's are cryin' (*3 times*)
Because their mammy's dead.

Go tell Aunt Rhody (*3 times*)
That the old gray goose is dead.

19

The Old Gray Mare

Oh, the old gray mare, she ain't what she used to be, Ain't what she used to be,

ain't what she used to be. The old gray mare, she ain't what she used to be,

Man-y long years a - go. *Chorus* Man-y long years a - go,

man - y long years a - go. The old gray mare, she

ain't what she used to be, Man - y long years a - go.

E-ri-e Canal

19th Century American Folk Song

We were loaded down with barley,
We were chock full up on rye,
And the captain he looked down at me
With his God damn' wicked eye.
Chorus

The captain he came up on deck
With a spyglass in his hand.
And the fog it was so gosh-darn thick,
That he could not spy the land.
Chorus

Two days out of Syracuse
Our vessel struck a shoal,
And we like to all been drownded
On a chunk o' Lackawanna coal.
Chorus

Our cook she was a grand old gal,
She wore a ragged dress.
We hoisted her upon a pole
As a signal of distress.
Chorus

The captain, he got married,
And the cook, she went to jail.
And I'm the only son of a gun
That's left to tell the tale.
Chorus

21

Home On The Range

How often at night when the heavens are bright
With the light from the glittering stars,
Have I stood there amazed and asked as I gazed,
If their glory exceeds that of ours.

Where the air is so pure, the zephyrs so free,
The breezes so balmy and light,
That I would not exchange my home on the range
For all of the cities so bright.

Oh, I love those wild flow'rs in this dear land of ours,
The curlew, I love to hear scream,
And I love the white rocks and the antelope flocks,
That graze on the mountaintops green.

The Yellow Rose Of Texas

Civil War

There's a yel - low rose in Tex - as that I am going to see, No

oth - er sol - dier knows her, no sol - dier, on - ly me; She

cried so when I left her, it like to broke my heart, And

if I ev - er find her, we nev - er more will part.

Chorus:
She's the sweetest rose of color this soldier ever knew,
Her eyes are bright as diamonds, they sparkle like the dew;
You may talk about your dearest May and sing of Rosa Lee,
But the Yellow Rose of Texas beats the belles of Tennessee.

Where the Rio Grande is flowing and the starry skies are bright,
She walks along the river in the quiet summer night;
She thinks if I remember, when we parted long ago,
I promised to come back again and not to leave her so. *Chorus*

Oh, now I'm going to find her, for my heart is full of woe,
And we'll sing the song together, that we sung so long ago;
We'll play the banjo gaily, and we'll sing the songs of yore,
And the Yellow Rose of Texas shall be mine forevermore. *Chorus*

When Johnny Comes Marching Home

Civil War

Get ready for the Jubilee. . .
We'll give the hero three times three. . .
The laurel wreath is ready now
To place upon his loyal brow. . .

The old church bell will peal with joy. . .
To welcome home our darling boy. . .
The village lads and lassies say,
With roses they will strew the way. . .

Let love and friendship on that day. . .
Their choicest treasures then display. . .
And let each one perform some part,
To fill with joy the warrior's heart. . .

Bile Them Cabbage Down

Southern Folk Song

Lively

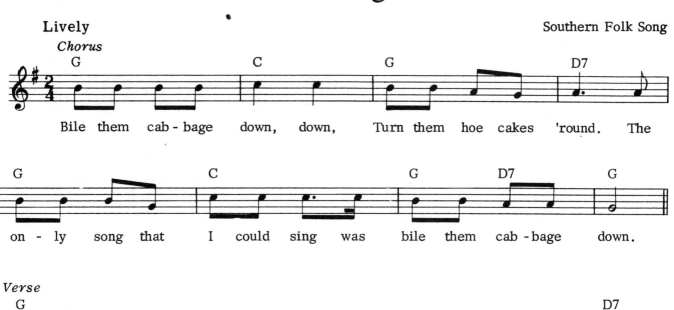

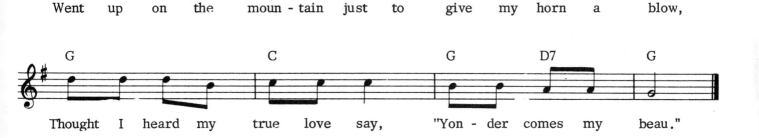

Took my gal to the blacksmith shop
To have her mouth made small,
She turned around a time or two
And swallowed shop and all.
Chorus

Possum in a 'simmon tree,
Raccoon on the ground,
Raccoon says, "You son-of-a-gun,
Shake some 'simmons down!"
Chorus

Someone stole my old 'coon dog,
Wish they'd bring him back,
He chased the big hogs through the fence
And the little ones through the crack.
Chorus

Met a possum in the road,
Blind as he could be,
Jumped the fence and whipped my dog
And bristled up at me.
Chorus

Once I had an old gray mule,
His name was Simon Slick,
He'd roll his eyes and back his ears,
And how that mule would kick.
Chorus

How that mule would kick!
He kicked with his dying breath;
He shoved his hind feet down his throat
And kicked himself to death.
Chorus

Down In The Valley

Southern Prison Folk Song

Down in the val - ley,_____ Val - ley so

low,_____ Hang your head o -

ver,_____ Hear the wind blow._____

Hear the wind blow, love, hear the wind blow,
Hang you head over, hear the wind blow.

If you don't love me, love whom you please.
Throw your arms 'round me, give my heart ease.

Give my heart ease, love, give my heart ease,
Throw your arms 'round me, give my heart ease.

Write me a letter, send it by mail,
Send it in care of the Birmingham Jail.

Birmingham Jail, love, Birmingham Jail,
Send it in care of the Birmingham Jail.

Build me a castle forty feet high,
So I can see her as she rides by.

As she rides by, love, as she rides by,
So I can see her as she rides by.

Roses love sunshine, violets love dew,
Angels in heaven know I love you.

Know I love you, dear, know I love you,
Angels in heaven know I love you.

Cindy

Southern Mountain Folk Song

Fast: Square Dance tempo

Oh, have you seen my Cin - dy, She

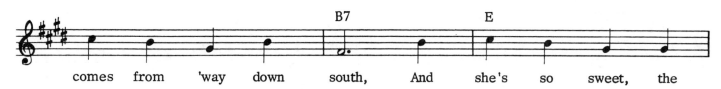

comes from 'way down south, And she's so sweet, the

hon - ey bees just swarm a - round her mouth.

Chorus

Get a - long home, Cin - dy, Cin - dy, Get a - long

home, Cin - dy, Cin - dy, Get a - long home, Cin - dy,

Cin - dy, I'll mar - ry you some day.

I wish I was an apple,
A-hangin' in a tree,
And ev'ry time my sweetheart passed,
She's take a bite of me.
Chorus

She told me that she loved me,
She called me sugar plum,
She throwed 'er arms around me,
I thought my time had come.
Chorus

She took me to the parlor,
She cooled me with her fan.
She swore I was the purtiest thing
In the shape of mortal man.
Chorus

I wish I had a needle,
As fine as I could sew,
I'd sew the girls to my coat tail,
And down the road I'd go.
Chorus

Cindy got religion,
She had it once before;
But when she heard my old banjo,
She 'uz the first un on the floor.
Chorus

Cindy went to the preachin',
She swung around and around;
She got so full of glory,
She knocked the preacher down.
Chorus

27

No Hiding Place

Spiritual

No hid - ing place down there,— No hid - ing place down there,— Went to the rock to hide my face, The rock cried out, "No hid - ing place." No hid - ing place down there.—

The rock cried, "I'm burning too."
The rock cried, "I'm burning too."
Oh, the rock cried out, "I'm burning too,
I want to go to heaven the same as you."
There's no hiding place down here.

Shady Grove

Southern Banjo Folk Song

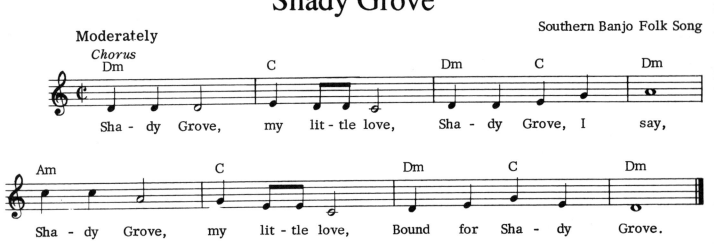

Sha - dy Grove, my lit - tle love, Sha - dy Grove, I say, Sha - dy Grove, my lit - tle love, Bound for Sha - dy Grove.

Wish I was in Shady Grove,
Sittin' in a rockin' chair,
And if those blues would bother me
I'd rock away from there.
Chorus

When you go to catch a fish,
Fish with a hook and line.
When you go to court a girl,
Never look back behind.
Chorus

When I was a little boy,
All I wanted was a knife.
Now I am a great big boy,
I'm a-lookin' for a wife.
Chorus

Sail Away, Ladies

Southern Banjo Folk Song

Moderately fast

If ev - er I get my new house done, Sail a - way, la - dies,

sail a - way, I'll give my old one to my son,

Sail a - way, la - dies, sail a - way. *Chorus* Don't she rock 'em, die - di - o,

Don't she rock 'em, die - di - o, Don't she rock___ 'em,

die - di - o, Don't she rock 'em, die - di - o.

Children, don't you grieve and cry,
  Sail away, ladies, sail away,
You're gonna be angels by and by.
  Sail away, ladies, sail away.
Chorus

Come along, girls, and go with me,
  Sail away, ladies, sail away,
We'll go back to Tennessee.
  Sail away, ladies, sail away.
Chorus

I got a letter from Shiloh town,
  Sail away, ladies, sail away,
Big Saint Louie is a-burning down,
  Sail away, ladies, sail away.
Chorus

I chew my tobacco and I spit my juice,
  Sail away, ladies, sail away,
I love my own daughter but it ain't no use,
  Sail away, ladies, sail away.
Chorus

All My Trials

American Folk Song

I had a little book, 'twas given to me,
And every page spelled "Victory."
All my trials, Lord, soon be over.
Chorus

Hush, little baby, don't you cry,
You know your momma was born to die.
All my trials, Lord, soon be over.
Chorus

Wade In The Water

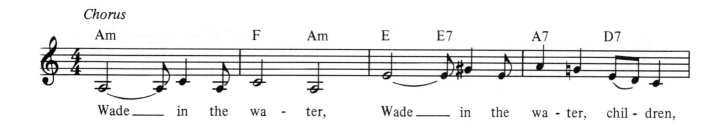

Chorus

Wade — in the wa - ter, Wade — in the wa - ter, chil - dren,

Wade — in the wa - ter, God's a - gon - na trou - ble the wa - ter.

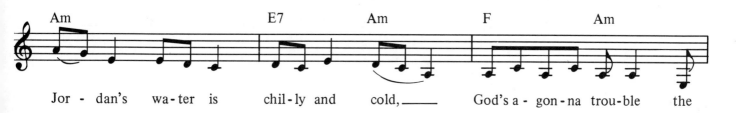

Jor - dan's wa - ter is chil - ly and cold, — God's a - gon - na trou - ble the

wa - ter. It chills — the bod - y, but lifts up the soul, —

God's a - gon - na trou - ble the wa - ter.

Jordsn's water is deep and wide,   If you get there before I do,
God's a-gonna trouble the water.   God's a-gonna trouble the water.
Meet my mother on the other side,   Tell all of my friends I'm coming too,
God's a-gonna trouble the water. *Chorus* God's a-gonna trouble the water. *Chorus*

Jacob's Ladder

Spiritual

Slow hymn

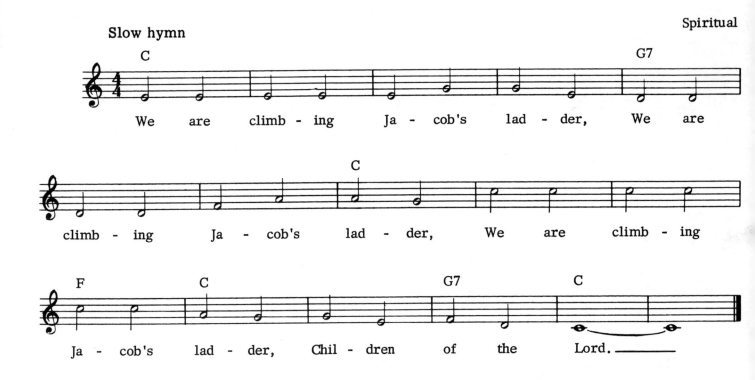

Every rung goes higher and higher,
Every rung goes higher and higher,
Every rung goes higher and higher,
Children of the Lord.

Every new man makes us stronger,
Every new man makes us stronger,
Every new man makes us stronger,
Children of the Lord.

We have toiled in dark and danger,
We have toiled in dark and danger,
We have toiled in dark and danger,
Children of the Lord.

Repeat Verse One

Battle Hymn Of The Republic

Julia Ward Howe
1861

Bold, Marching Tempo

1. Mine eyes have seen the glo - ry of the com - ing of the Lord; He is tramp - ling out the vin - tage where the grapes of wrath are stored; He has loosed the fate - ful light - ning of His ter - ri - ble swift sword, His Truth is march - ing on.

CHORUS

Glo - ry, glo - ry, Hal - le - lu - jah! Glo - ry, glo - ry, Hal - le - lu - jah! Glo - ry, glo - ry! Hal - le - lu - jah! His Truth is march - ing on.

I have seen Him in the watch-fires of a hundred circling camps;
They have builded Him an altar in the evening dews and damps;
I can read His righteous sentence by the dim and flaring lamps,
His day is marching on. *Chorus*

33

John Brown's Body

Based on "The Battle Hymn of the Republic"

March tempo

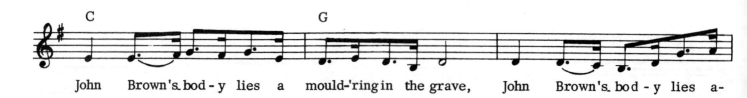

John Brown's_ bod - y lies a mould-'ring in the grave,

John Brown's bod-y lies a mould-'ring in the grave, John Brown's bod-y lies a-

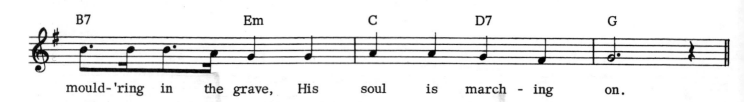

mould-'ring in the grave, His soul is march - ing on.

Chorus

Glo - ry, glo - ry, hal - le - lu - jah! Glo - ry, glo - ry, hal - le - lu - jah!

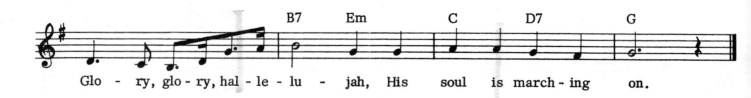

Glo - ry, glo - ry, hal - le - lu - jah, His soul is march - ing on.

He captured Harper's Ferry with his nineteen men so true,
And he frightened old Virginia 'til she trembled through and through.
They hung him for a traitor, they themselves the traitor crew,
  But his soul is marching on!
Chorus

John Brown died that the slave might be free,
John Brown died that the slave might be free,
John Brown died that the slave might be free,
  And his soul is marching on!
Chorus

The stars of Heaven are looking kindly down,
The stars of Heaven are looking kindly down,
The stars of Heaven are looking kindly down,
  On the grave of old John Brown.
Chorus

Now has come the glorious jubilee,
Now has come the glorious jubilee,
Now has come the glorious jubilee,
  When all mankind are free.
Chorus

The Marines' Hymn

From the Halls of Mon - te - zu_____ ma, to the shores of

Tri - po - li,_____ We__ fight our coun - try's bat - tles on the

land as on the sea._____ First to fight for right and free___

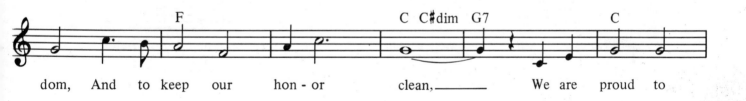

dom, And to keep our hon - or clean,_____ We are proud to

claim the tit - tle of U - nit - ed States Ma - rines._____

Our flag's unfurled to every breeze
From dawn to setting sun.
We have fought in every clime and place
Where we could take a gun.
In the snow of far-off Northern lands
And in sunny Tropic scenes,
You will find us always on the job -
The United States Marines.

Here's health to you and to our Corps
Which we are proud to serve.
In many a strife we've fought for life
And never lost our nerve.
If the Army and the Navy
Ever look on Heaven's scenes,
They will find the streets are guarded
By United States Marines.

For He's A Jolly Good Fellow

For___ he's a jol-ly good fel - low, for he's a jol-ly good fel - low, for
he's a jol-ly good fel - low, which no - one can de - ny.___ Which no - one can de -
ny, ___ Which no - one can de - ny,___ For he's a jol-ly good fel - low, for
he's a jol-ly good fel - low, for he's a jol-ly good fel - low, And so say all of us.

The Caissons Go Rolling Along

O - ver hill, o - ver dale, as we hit the dust - y trail
out, hear them shout, coun - ter march and right a - bout } As the
cais - sons go march-ing a - long._____ In and __ Then it's
Hi! Hi! Hee! in the field Ar - til - ler - y, shout out your
num - bers loud and strong!_____ For where - 'er you go,
You will al - ways know that the cais - sons are roll - ings a - long._____

She'll Be Comin' Round The Mountain

Play-Party Song

She'll be riding six white horses when she comes,
She'll be riding six white horses when she comes,
She'll be riding six white horses, she'll be riding six white horses,
She'll be riding six white horses when she comes.

Oh, we'll all go out to meet her when she comes,
Oh, we'll all go out to meet her when she comes,
Oh, we'll all go out to meet her and we'll all be glad to greet her,
Oh, we'll all go out to meet her when she comes,

Oh, we'll kill the old red rooster when she comes,
Oh, we'll kill the old red rooster when she comes,
Oh, we'll kill the old red rooster 'cause he don't crow like he uster,
Oh, we'll kill the old red rooster when she comes,

My Home's Across The Smoky Mountains

Moderately fast

Southern Mountain Folk Song

My home's a - cross the Smo - ky Moun -

tains, My home's a - cross the Smo - ky Moun -

tains, My home's a - cross the Smo - ky

Moun - tains, And I'll nev - er get to

see you an - y more, more, more, And I'll

nev - er get to see you an - y more.

Good-bye, honey, sugar darling,
Good-bye, honey, sugar darling,
Good-bye, honey, sugar darling,
And I'll never get to see you any more, more, more,
I'll never get to see you any more.

Rock my honey, feed her candy,
Rock my honey, feed her candy,
Rock my honey, feed her candy,
And I'll never get to see you any more, more, more,
And I'll never get to see you any more.

Repeat Verse One

38

Michael, Row The Boat Ashore

Georgia Sea Islands Folk Song

Moderately

Mi - chael, row the boat a - shore, Al - le - lu -

ya, Mi - chael, row the boat a - shore, Al - le - lu - ya.

Sister, help to trim the sail,
   Hallelujah!
Sister, help to trim the sail,
   Hallelujah!

Jordan's River is chilly and cold,
   Hallelujah!
Chills the body but not the soul,
   Hallelujah!

Jordan's River is deep and wide,
   Hallelujah!
Milk and honey on the other side,
   Hallelujah!

I have heard the good news too,
   Hallelujah!
I have heard the good news too,
   Hallelujah!

Repeat Verse One

Pay Me My Money Down

West Indian Folk Song

With a bounce

Chorus

Pay me,_ oh, pay me,_ Pay me my mon - ey down,_

Pay me or go to jail,_ Pay me my mon - ey down._

I thought I heard the captain say,
Pay me my money down.
Tomorrow is our sailing day,
Pay me my money down.
Chorus

The very next day we cleared the bar...
He knocked me down with the end of a spar...
Chorus

I wish I was Mister Howard's son...
Sit in the house and drink all the rum...
Chorus

I wish I was Mister Steven's son...
Sit in the shade and watch all the work done...
Chorus

There's lots more verses to this song...
But I guess we better be moving along...
Chorus

Rise And Shine

Children's Song

Jubilantly

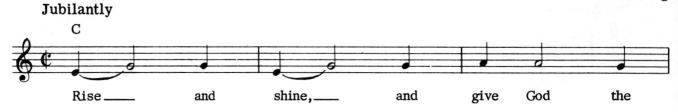

Rise____ and shine,____ and give God the

glo - ry, glo - ry, Rise____ and shine,__ and give God the

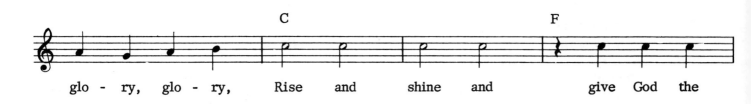

glo - ry, glo - ry, Rise and shine and give God the

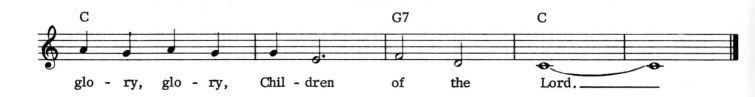

glo - ry, glo - ry, Chil - dren of the Lord._____

The Lord said, "Noah, there's gonna be a floody, floody."
The Lord said, "Noah, there's gonna be a floody, floody.
Get your children out of the muddy, muddy!"
Children of the Lord.

Noah, he built him, he built him an arky, arky,
Noah, he built him, he built him an arky, arky,
Make it out of hickory barky, barky,
Children of the Lord.

The animals, they came, they came by twosy, twosy,
The animals, they came, they came by twosy, twosy,
Elephants and kangaroosy, roosy.
Children of the Lord.

It rained and rained for forty daysy, daysy,
It rained and rained for forty daysy, daysy,
Drove those animals nearly crazy, crazy,
Children of the Lord.

Repeat Verse One

On Top Of Old Smoky

Southern Mountain Folk Song

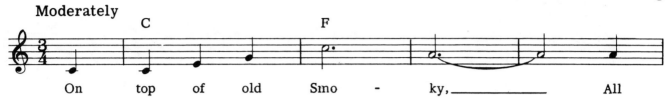

On top of old Smo - ky, _____ All

cov - ered with snow, _____ I lost my true lov -

er, _____ By a - court - in' too slow. _____

Well, a-courting's a pleasure,
And parting is grief;
But a false-hearted lover
Is worse than a thief.

A thief he will rob you
And take all you have,
But a false-hearted lover
Will send you to your grave.

And the grave will decay you
And turn you to dust,
And where is the young man
A poor girl can trust.

They'll hug you and kiss you
And tell you more lies
Than the cross-ties on the railroad,
Or the stars in the skies.

They'll tell you they love you,
Just to give your heart ease;
But the minute your back's turned,
They'll court whom they please.

So come all you young maidens
And listen to me.
Never place your affection
On a green willow tree.

For the leaves they will wither
And the roots they will die,
And your true love will leave you,
And you'll never know why.

This Little Light Of Mine

On Mon-day he gave me the gift of love, On

Tues-day peace came from a-bove, On Wednes-day told me to

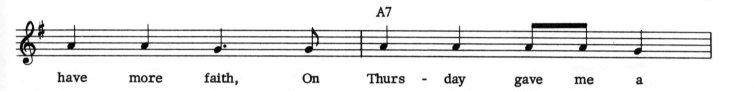

have more faith, On Thurs-day gave me a

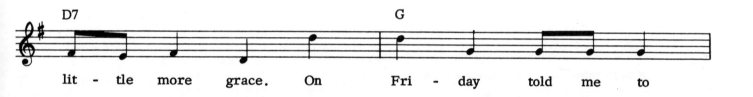

lit-tle more grace. On Fri-day told me to

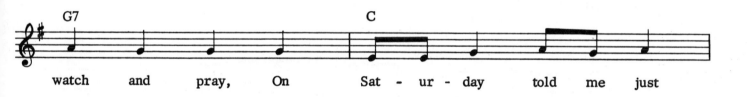

watch and pray, On Sat-ur-day told me just

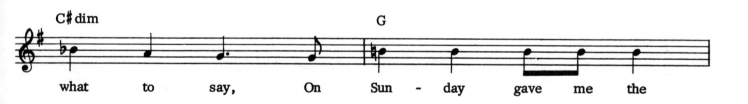

what to say, On Sun-day gave me the

pow-er di-vine, Just to let my lit-tle light shine. Oh

43

The Titanic

American Folk Song

Oh, they sailed from England's shore
'Bout a thousand miles or more,
When the rich refused to associate with the poor,
So they put them down below,
Where they'd be the first to go,
It was sad when that great ship went down.
Chorus

Oh, the boat was full of sin,
And the sides about to burst,
When the captain shouted, "Women and children first!"
Oh, the captain tried to wire,
But the lines were all on fire,
It was sad when that great ship went down.
Chorus

Oh, they swung the lifeboats out
O'er the deep and raging sea,
And the band struck up with "A-Nearer, My God to Thee."
Little children wept and cried,
As the waves swept o'er the side,
It was sad when that great ship went down.
Chorus

Deep Blue Sea

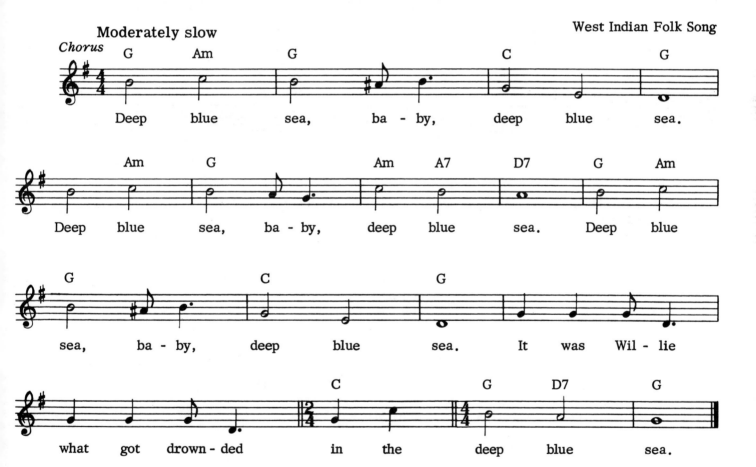

Moderately slow

West Indian Folk Song

Deep blue sea, ba - by, deep blue sea.
Deep blue sea, ba - by, deep blue sea. Deep blue
sea, ba - by, deep blue sea. It was Wil - lie
what got drown - ded in the deep blue sea.

Dig his grave with a silver spade,
Dig his grave with a silver spade,
Dig his grave with a silver spade,
It was Willie what got drownded in the deep blue sea.
Chorus

Lower him down with a golden chain, (*3 times*)
It was Willie what got drownded in the deep blue sea.
Chorus

Golden sun bring him back again, (*3 times*)
It was Willie what got drownded in the deep blue sea.
Chorus

Everybody Loves Saturday Night

Nigerian Folk Song

With a Calypso beat

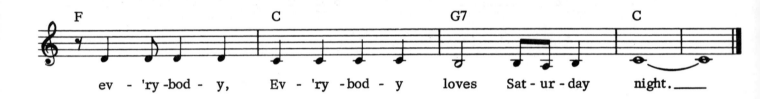

NIGERIAN:	Bobo waro fero Satodeh,
	Bobo waro fero Satodeh,
	Bobo waro, bobo waro,
	Bobo waro fero Satodeh.
FRENCH:	Tout le monde aime Samedi soir.
YIDDISH:	Jeder eyne hot lieb Shabas ba nacht.
CHINESE:	Ren ren si huan li pai lu.
RUSSIAN:	Vsiem nravitsa subbota vietcherom.
CZECH:	Kazhdi ma rad sabotu vietcher.
SPANISH:	A todos les gusta la noche del Sabado.
ITALIAN:	Tutti vogliono il sabato sera.

Gee, But I Want To Go Home

World War I U. S. Army Folk Song

The cof-fee that they give you, they say is might-y fine, It's

good for cuts and bruis-es, And it tastes like i - o - dine.

Chorus

I don't want no more of ar - my life, Gee, but I want to go home.

The biscuits that they give you they say are mighty fine;
One rolled off a table and it killed a pal of mine.
Chorus

The chickens that they give you they say are mighty fine;
One rolled off a table and it started marking time.
Chorus

The details that they give us they say are mighty fine;
The garbage that we pick up they feed us all the time.
Chorus

The clothes that they give you they say are mighty fine;
But me and my buddy can both fit into mine.
Chorus

The women in the service club they say are mighty fine;
But most are over ninety and the rest are under nine.
Chorus

They treat us all like monkeys and make us stand in line;
They give you fifty dollars and take back forty-nine.
Chorus

Putting On The Style

American Folk Song

Lively

Young man in a car - riage, driv - ing like he's mad,

With a pair of hors - es he's bor - rowed from his dad. He

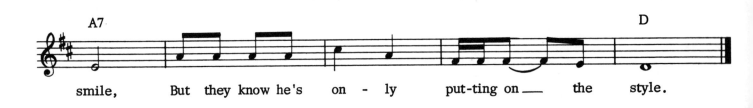

cracks his whip so live - ly, Just to make the la - dies

smile, But they know he's on - ly put-ting on ___ the style.

Chorus: Putting on the agony,
Putting on the style,
That's what all the young folks
Are doing all the while.
And as I look around me
I'm very apt to smile,
To see so many people
Putting on the style.

Sweet sixteen and goes to church
Just to see the boys,
Laughs and giggles
At every little noise.
She turns this way a little,
And turns that way a while,
But everybody knows she's only
Putting on the style.
Chorus

Young man just from college
Makes a big display
With a great big jawbreak,
Which he can hardly say.
It can't be found in Webster's,
And won't be for a while,
But everybody knows he's only
Putting on the style.
Chorus

48

A Bicycle Built For Two

Words and Music by
Harry Dacre

Dai - sy, Dai - sy, give me your an - swer, do.____ I'm half cra - zy all for the love of you.____ It won't be a styl - ish mar - riage,____ I can't of ford a car - riage.____ But you'll look sweet up - on the seat of a bi - cy - cle built for two.____

Reuben And Rachel

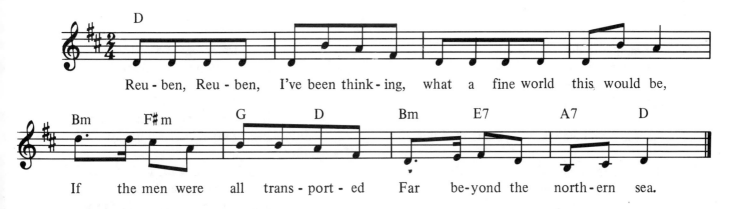

Reu - ben, Reu - ben, I've been think - ing, what a fine world this would be, If the men were all trans - port - ed Far be-yond the north - ern sea.

Oh, my goodness, gracious Rachel,
What a queer world this would be,
If the men were all transported
Far beyond the northern sea.

Reuben, Reuben, I've been thinking,
What a gay life girls would lead,
If they had no men about them,
None to tease them, none to heed.

Reuben, Reuben, stop your teasing,
If you've any love for me,
I was only just a-fooling,
As I thought, of course, you'd see.

Rachel, if you'll not transport us,
I will take you for my wife,
And I'll split with you my money
Every pay-day of my life.

The Boll Weevil

Southern Folk Song

Moderately

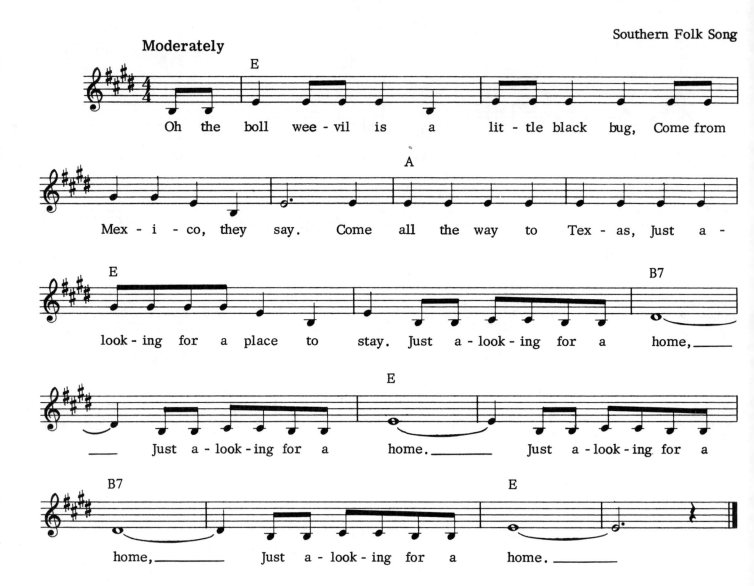

Oh the boll wee-vil is a lit-tle black bug, Come from Mex-i-co, they say. Come all the way to Tex-as, Just a-look-ing for a place to stay. Just a-look-ing for a home,_____ _____ Just a-look-ing for a home._____ Just a-look-ing for a home,_____ Just a-look-ing for a home._____

The first time I seen the boll weevil,
He was sitting on the square.
The next time I seen the boll weevil,
He had all his family there...
Just a-looking for a home, just a-looking for a home.
Just a-looking for a home, just a-looking for a home.

The farmer said to the weevil,
"What makes your face so red?"
The weevil said to the farmer,
"It's a wonder I ain't dead..."
Just a-looking for a home, just a-looking for a home.
Just a-looking for a home, just a-looking for a home.

The farmer took the boll weevil,
And he put him in hot sand.
The weevil said, "This is mighty hot,
But I'll stand it like a man.
This'll be my home, this'll be my home.
This'll be my home, this'll be my home."

The farmer took the boll weevil,
And he put him in a lump of ice.
The boll weevil said to the farmer,
"This is mighty cool and nice,
It'll be my home, it'll be my home.
It'll be my home, it'll be my home."

The farmer took the boll weevil,
And he put him in the fire.
The boll weevil said to the farmer,
"This is just what I desire,
This'll be my home, this'll be my home.
This'll be my home, this'll be my home."

The boll weevil said to the farmer,
"You better leave me alone;
I ate up all your cotton,
And I'm starting on your corn.
I'll have a home, I'll have a home.
I'll have a home, I'll have a home."

The merchant got half the cotton,
The boll weevil got the rest.
Didn't leave the farmer's wife
But one old cotton dress,
And it's full of holes, and it's full of holes.
And it's full of holes, and it's full of holes.

The farmer said to the merchant,
"We're in an awful fix;
The boll weevil ate all the cotton up
And left us only sticks.
We got no home, we got no home.
We got no home, we got no home."

The farmer said to the merchant,
"We ain't made but one bale,
And before we'll give you that one,
We'll fight and go to jail...
We'll have a home, we'll have a home.
We'll have a home, we'll have a home."

Green Corn

Fast

Play Party Folk Song

Green corn, come a - long, Chol - ly, Green corn, don't-cha tell Pol - ly, All I need in this cre - a - tion, Pret - ty lit - tle wife and a big plan - ta - tion.

All I need to make me happy,
Two little kids to call me pappy.
Chorus

One named Bill, the other Davy,
They like their biscuits slopped in gravy.
Chorus

All I need in this creation,
Three months work and nine vacation.
Chorus

Tell my boss any old time,
Daytime's his but nighttime's mine.
Chorus

51

What Shall We Do With The Drunken Sailor?

British Sailor's Folk Song

Rousingly

What shall we do with the drunk - en sail - or?

What shall we do with the drunk - en sail - or? What shall we do with the

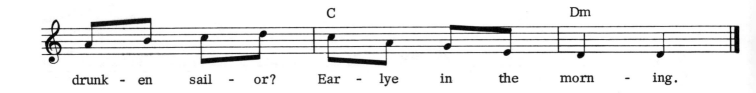

drunk - en sail - or? Ear - lye in the morn - ing.

Chorus: Hooray, and up she rises,
Hooray, and up she rises,
Hooray, and up she rises,
Earlye in the morning.

Put him in the scuppers with a hose pipe on him, (*3 times*)
Earlye in the morning.
Chorus

Heave him by the leg in a running bowline, (*3 times*)
Earlye in the morning.
Chorus

Shave his belly with a rusty razor, (*3 times*)
Earlye in the morning.
Chorus

That's what we'll do with the drunken sailor, (*3 times*)
Earlye in the morning.
Chorus

Joshua Fought The Battle Of Jericho

Up to the walls of Jericho
He marched with spear in hand;
"Go blow them ram horns," Joshua cried,
" 'Cause the battle is in my hand!"
Chorus

Then the lamb ram sheep horns begin to blow,
Trumpets begin to sound,
Joshua commanded the children to shout,
And the walls came tumble-ing down!
Chorus

Red River Valley

American Folk Song

Moderately

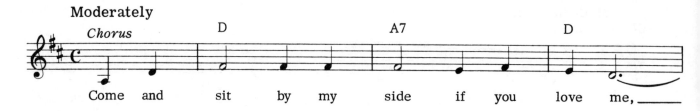

Chorus

Come and sit by my side if you love me, ___

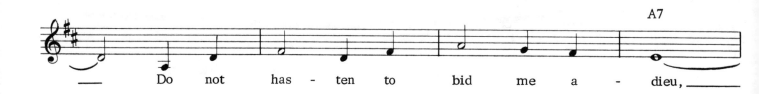

___ Do not has - ten to bid me a - dieu, ___

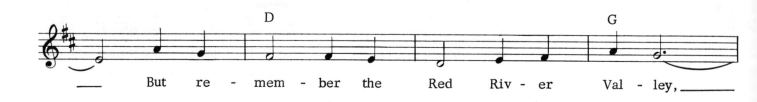

___ But re - mem - ber the Red Riv - er Val - ley, ___

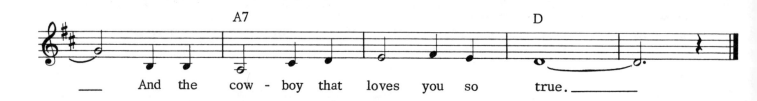

___ And the cow - boy that loves you so true. ___

Won't you think of this valley you're leaving,
Oh, how lonely, how sad it will be,
Oh, think of the fond heart you're breaking,
And the grief you are causing me.
Chorus

From this valley they say you are going,
When you go may your darling go, too?
Would you leave her behind unprotected
When she loves no other but you?
Chorus

Old Joe Clark

Southern Fiddle Folk Song

Lively

Old Joe Clark, the preach-er's son, Preached all o - ver the

plain, The on - ly text he ev - er used was

"High, low, jack and the game." Round and a - round, Old Joe Clark,

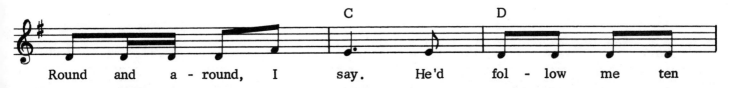

Round and a - round, I say. He'd fol - low me ten

thou - sand miles, To hear my fid - dle play.

I used to live on mountain-top,
But now I live in town.
I'm boarding at the big hotel,
Courting Betsy Brown.
Chorus

When I was a little girl,
I used to play with toys;
Now I am a bigger girl,
I'd rather play with boys.
Chorus

When I was a little boy,
I used to want a knife;
Now I am a bigger boy,
I only want a wife.
Chorus

Wish I was a sugar tree,
Standin' in the middle of some town;
Ev'ry time a pretty girl passed,
I'd shake some sugar down.
Chorus

Old Joe had a yellow cat,
She would not sing or pray;
She stuck her head in a buttermilk jar
And washed her sins away.
Chorus

I wish I had a sweetheart;
I'd set her on the shelf,
And ev'rytime she'd smile at me
I'd get up there myself.
Chorus

Home In That Rock

Spiritual

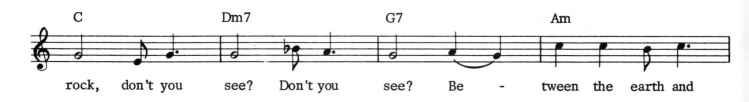

Poor man Lazarus, poor as I, don't you see? Don't you see?
Poor man Lazarus, poor as I, don't you see? Don't you see?
Poor man Lazarus, poor as I,
When he died he found a Home on High,
He had a Home in that Rock, don't you see?

Rich man Dives lived so well, don't you see? Don't you see?
Rich man Dives lived so well, don't you see? Don't you see?
Rich man Dives lived so well,
When he died he found a Home in Hell,
Had no Home in-a that Rock, don't you see?

God gave Noah the rainbow sign, don't you see? Don't you see?
God gave Noah the rainbow sign, don't you see? Don't you see?
God gave Noah the rainbow sign,
No more water — but fire next time,
Noah had a Home in that Rock, don't you see?

Do, Lord

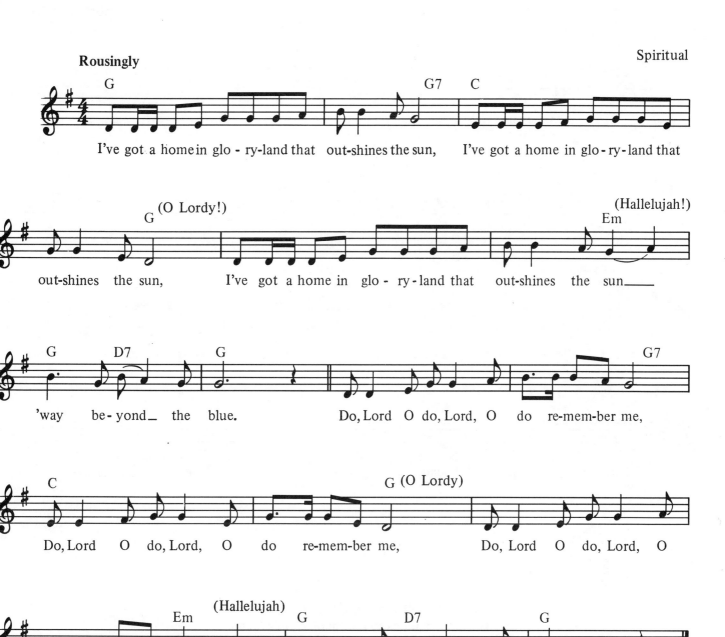

Rousingly

Spiritual

I've got a home in glo-ry-land that out-shines the sun, I've got a home in glo-ry-land that

out-shines the sun, (O Lordy!) I've got a home in glo-ry-land that out-shines the sun___ (Hallelujah!)

'way be-yond___ the blue. Do, Lord O do, Lord, O do re-mem-ber me,

Do, Lord O do, Lord, O do re-mem-ber me, Do, Lord O do, Lord, O (O Lordy)

do re-mem-ber me_____ (Hallelujah) 'way be-yond the blue.

This Train

American Folk Song

This train is bound for glo-ry, this train,_____

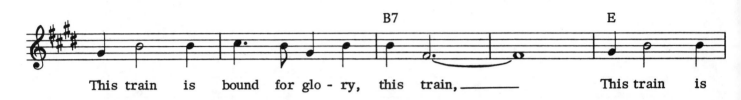

This train is bound for glo-ry, this train,_____ This train is

bound for glo-ry, Don't ride noth-in' but the right-eous and the ho-ly.

This train is bound for glo-ry, this train._____

This train don't carry no gamblers, this train.
This train don't carry no gamblers, this train.
This train don't carry no gamblers,
No hypocrites, no midnight ramblers,
This train is bound for glory, this train.

This train is built for speed now, this train (*3 times*)
Fastest train you every did see,
This train is bound for glory, this train.

This train don't carry no liars, this train (*3 times*)
No hypocrites and no high flyers,
This train is bound for glory, this train.

Rock – A – My Soul

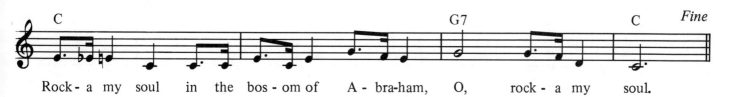

Rock-a-my soul in the bos-om of A-bra-ham, Rock-a my soul in the bos-om of A-bra-ham,

Rock-a my soul in the bos-om of A-bra-ham, O, rock-a my soul.

When I went down to the val-ley to pray, O, rock-a my soul, My

soul got hap-py and I stayed_ all day, O, rock-a my soul.

When I was a mourner just like you,
O, rock-a my soul,
I mourned and I mourned till I come through,
O, rock-a my soul, *Chorus*

Scotland's Burning

4-part round

Scot-land's burn-ing, Scot-land's burn-ing! Look out! look out!

Fire! fire! fire! fire! Pour on wa-ter, pour on wa-ter.

59

Comin' Through The Rye

Scotland

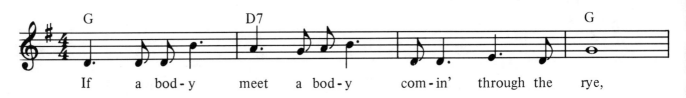

If a bod-y meet a bod-y com-in' through the rye,

If a bod-y kiss a bod-y, need a bod-y cry?

Ev - 'ry las-sie has a lad-die, None, they say, ha'e I, Yet

a' the lads they smile on me, When com-in' through the rye.

Gin a body meet a body,
Comin' frae the toon,
Gin a body greet a body,
Need a body froon?
Among the train there is a swain,
I dearly love mysel;
But what's his name or what's his hame,
I donna care to tell.

Loch Lomond

Words and Lady John Scott
Scotland

By___ yon bon - nie banks and by yon bon - nie braes, Where the

sun shines__ bright on Loch Lo - mond, Where me and my true love were
I'll be in Scot - land be - fore you. But me and my true love will

ev - er wont to be
nev - er meet a - gain } On the bon-nie, bon-nie banks of Loch Lo - mond,

Chorus

Oh, you'll take the high road and I'll take the low road, And

I mind where we parted in yon shady glen,
On the steep, steep side of Ben Lomond,
Where the deep purple hue the Highlands we view,
And the moon coming out in the gloaming. *Chorus*

The wee birdies sing and the wild flowers spring,
And in sunshine the waters are sleeping.
But the broken heart will ken no second spring again,
And the world does not know how we are greeting. *Chorus*

Bowling Green

Southern Banjo Folk Song

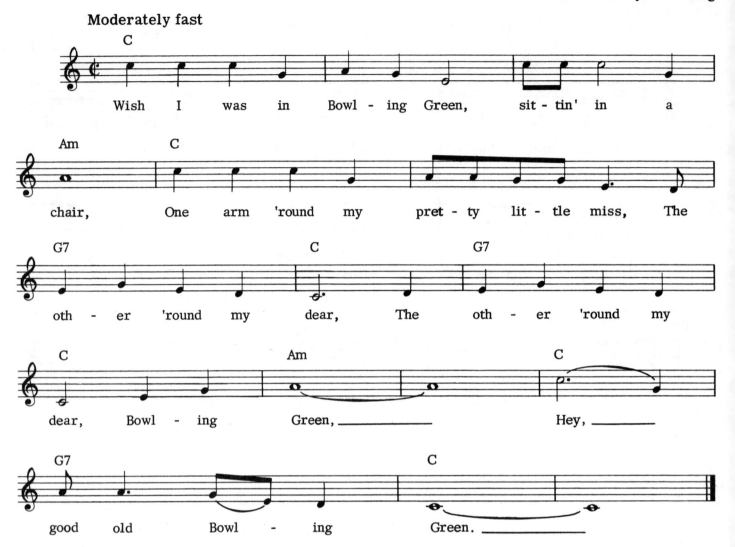

Moderately fast

Wish I was in Bowl - ing Green, sit - tin' in a chair, One arm 'round my pret - ty lit - tle miss, The oth - er 'round my dear, The oth - er 'round my dear, Bowl - ing Green, _____ Hey, _____ good old Bowl - ing Green. _____

If you see that gal of mine, tell her once for me,
If she loves another boy, yes, I'll set her free,
Yes, I'll set her free, Bowling Green,
Hey, good old Bowling Green.

Wish I was a bumblebee, sailing through the air,
Sail right down to my true love's side, touch her if you dare,
Touch her if you dare, Bowling Green,
Hey, good old Bowling Green.

Goin' through this whole wide world, I'm going through alone,
Goin' through this whole wide world, I ain't got no home,
I ain't got no home, Bowling Green,
Hey, good old Bowling Green.

Come And Go With Me

Spiritual

Rhythmically

Come and go with me to that land, come and go

with me to that land, Come and go with me to that

land where I'm bound. _____ Come and go with me to that

land, Come and go with me to that land. Come and go

with me to that land where I'm bound. _____

We can worship in that land, we can worship in that land,
We can worship in that land where we're bound.
We can worship in that land, we can worship in that land,
We can worship in that land where we're bound.

There is love in that land, there is love in that land,
There is love in that land where we're bound.
There is love in that land, there is love in that land,
There is love in that land where we're bound.

People are joyful in that land, people are joyful in that land,
People are joyful in that land where we're bound.
People are joyful in that land, people are joyful in that land,
People are joyful in that land where we're bound.

Repeat Verse One

Kumbaya

Negro Folk Song

Kum - ba - ya, my Lord, ____ kum - ba - ya, ____

Kum - ba - ya, my Lord, ____ kum - ba - ya, ____

Kum - ba - ya, my Lord, ____ kum - ba - ya, ____

Oh, Lord, kum - ba - ya. ____

Someone's singing, Lord, kumbaya,
Someone's singing, Lord, kumbaya,
Someone's singing, Lord, kumbaya,
Oh, Lord, kumbaya.

Someone's dancing, Lord, kumbaya,
Someone's dancing, Lord, kumbaya,
Someone's dancing, Lord, kumbaya,
Oh, Lord, kumbaya.

Someone's weeping, Lord, kumbaya,
Someone's weeping, Lord, kumbaya,
Someone's weeping, Lord, kumbaya,
Oh, Lord, kumbaya.

Someone's shouting, Lord, kumbaya,
Someone's shouting, Lord, kumbaya,
Someone's shouting, Lord, kumbaya,
Oh, Lord, kumbaya.

Someone's praying, Lord, kumbaya,
Someone's praying, Lord, kumbaya,
Someone's praying, Lord, kumbaya,
Oh, Lord, kumbaya.

Oh, Sinner Man

With a beat

Spiritual

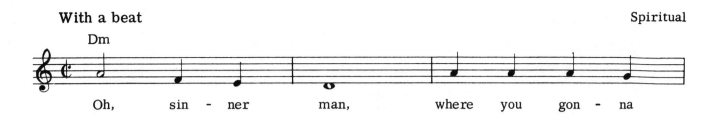

Oh, sin - ner man, where you gon - na

run to; Oh, sin - ner man, where you gon - na

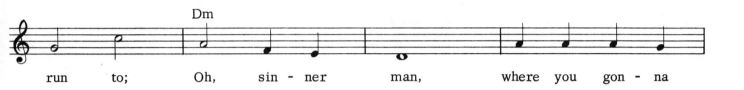

run to; Oh, sin - ner man, where you gon - na

run to, All on that day?_____

Run to the rock, the rock was a-melting,
Run to the rock, the rock was a-melting,
Run to the rock, the rock was a-melting,
All on that day.

Run to the sea, the sea was a-boiling, (*3 times*)
All on that day.

Run to the moon, the moon was a-bleeding, (*3 times*)
All on that day.

Run to the Lord, Lord won't you hide me? (*3 times*)
All on that day.

Run to the Devil, Devil was a-waiting, (*3 times*)
All on that day.

Oh sinner man, you oughta been a-praying, (*3 times*)
All on that day.

O Mary, Don't You Weep

Spiritual

Moses stood on the Red Sea shore,
Smitin' that water with a two-by-four.
   Pharaoh's army got drownded,
   Oh, Mary, don't you weep.
Chorus

God gave Noah the rainbow sign,
"No more water, but fire next time!"
   Pharaoh's army got drownded,
   Oh, Mary, don't you weep.
Chorus

One of these nights, about twelve o'clock,
This old world's gonna reel and rock.
   Pharaoh's army got drownded,
   Oh, Mary, don't you weep.
Chorus

I may be right and I may be wrong,
I know you're gonna miss me when I'm gone.
   Pharaoh's army got drownded,
   Oh, Mary, don't you weep.
Chorus

Worried Man Blues

Southern Folk Song

Moderately fast

It takes a wor-ried man to sing a wor-ried song, It takes a wor-ried man to sing a wor-ried song, It takes a wor-ried man to sing a wor-ried song, I'm wor-ried now,_____ but I won't be wor-ried long.

I went across the river, and I lay down to sleep, (*3 times*)
When I woke up, had shackles on my feet.

Twenty-nine links of chain around my leg, (*3 times*)
And on each link, an initial of my name.

I asked that judge, tell me, what's gonna be my fine? (*3 times*)
Twenty-one years on the Rocky Mountain Line.

Twenty-one years to pay my awful crime, (*3 times*)
Twenty-one years — but I got ninety-nine.

The train arrived sixteen coaches long, (*3 times*)
The girl I love is on that train and gone.

I looked down the track as far as I could see, (*3 times*)
Little bitty hand was waving after me.

If anyone should ask you who composed this song, (*3 times*)
Tell him was I, and I sing it all day long.

Take This Hammer

Slowly, with a heavy beat

Southern Chain Gang Folk Song

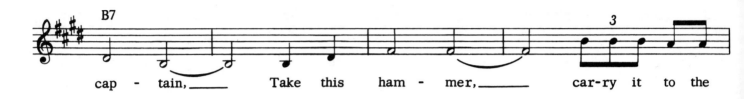

Take this ham - mer, _____ car - ry it to the

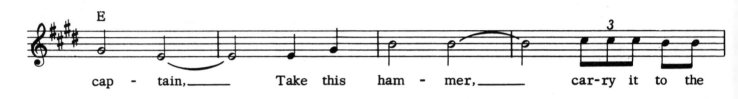

cap - tain, _____ Take this ham - mer, _____ car - ry it to the

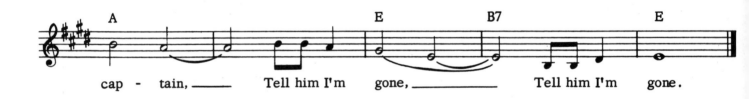

cap - tain, _____ Take this ham - mer, _____ car - ry it to the

cap - tain, _____ Tell him I'm gone, _____ Tell him I'm gone.

If he asks you, was I laughin',
If he asks you, was I laughin',
If he asks you, was I laughin',
Tell him I was cryin', tell him I was cryin'.

If he asks you, was I runnin',
If he asks you, was I runnin',
If he asks you, was I runnin',
Tell him I was flyin', tell him I was flyin'.

I don't want no cornbread and molasses,
I don't want no cornbread and molasses,
I don't want no cornbread and molasses,
They hurt my pride, they hurt my pride.

I don't want no cold iron shackles,
I don't want no cold iron shackles,
I don't want no cold iron shackles,
Around my leg, around my leg.

Repeat Verse One

Pick A Bale Of Cotton

Southern Folk Song

Gon - na jump down, turn a - round, Pick a bale of

cot - ton, Gon - na jump down, turn a - round,

Chorus

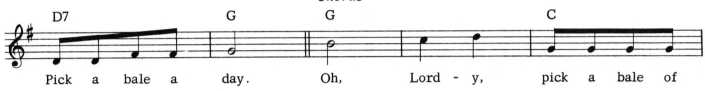

Pick a bale a day. Oh, Lord - y, pick a bale of

cot - ton, Oh, Lord - y, pick a bale a day.

Jump down, turn around, pick a bale of cotton,
Jump down, turn around, pick a bale a day.
Chorus

Me and my gal can pick a bale of cotton,
Me and my gal can pick a bale a day.
Chorus

Me and my wife can pick a bale of cotton,
Me and my wife can pick a bale a day.
Chorus

Me and my friend can pick a bale of cotton,
Me and my friend can pick a bale a day.
Chorus

My and my poppa can pick a bale of cotton,
My and my poppa can pick a bale a day.
Chorus

Down By The Riverside

Spiritual

Moderately fast

Gon - na lay down my sword and shield — Down by the
riv - er - side, — Down by the riv - er - side, —
Down by the riv - er - side, — Gon - na lay down my
sword and shield — Down by the riv - er - side, — And
stu - dy —— war no more. ——— I ain't gon - na

Chorus

stu - dy — war no more, I ain't gon - na stu - dy — war no

more, I ain't gon-na stu-dy _____ war no

1. more. _____ I ain't gon-na more.

2. more. _____

I'm gonna join hands with everyone,
Down by the riverside, down by the riverside,
Down by the riverside.
I'm gonna join hands with everyone,
Down by the riverside,
And study war no more.
Chorus

I'm gonna put on my long white robe...
Chorus

I'm gonna talk with the Prince of Peace...
Chorus

I'm gonna bury that atom bomb...
Chorus

When The Saints Go Marching In

Spiritual

Jubilantly

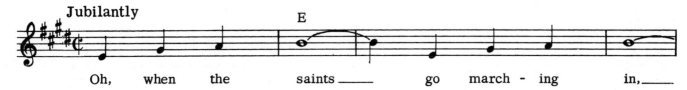

Oh, when the saints _____ go march-ing in, _____

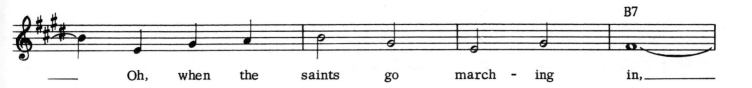

_____ Oh, when the saints go march-ing in, _____

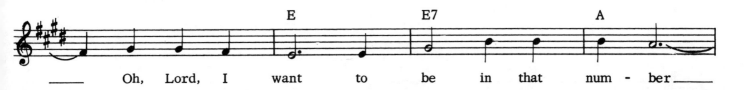

_____ Oh, Lord, I want to be in that num-ber _____

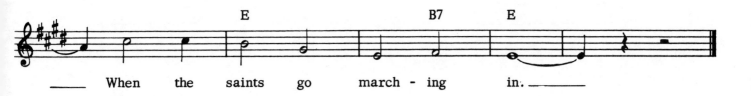

_____ When the saints go march-ing in. _____

And when the sun refuse to shine...

And when the moon drips red with blood...

And when the Revelation comes...

71

Jennie Jenkins

Children's Song

Moderately fast

(Boy) Will you wear white, Oh my dear, oh my dear, Oh,

will you wear white, Jen - ny Jenk - ins?_____

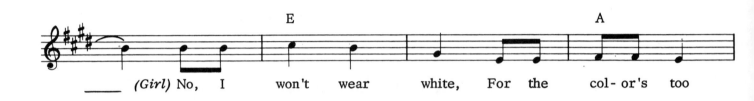

_____ (Girl) No, I won't wear white, For the col - or's too

bright. I'll___ buy me a fol - dy, rol - dy, til - dy, tol - dy,
(Together)

Seek a dou - ble, use a co - zy roll to find me.

Roll,_____ Jen - ny Jenk - ins, roll._____

Will you wear white, oh my dear, oh my dear?
Will you wear white, Jennie Jenkins?
  No, I won't wear white,
  For the color's too bright.
Chorus

Will you wear green, oh my dear, oh my dear?
Will you wear green, Jennie Jenkins?
  No, I won't wear green,
  It's a shame to be seen.
Chorus

Will you wear blue, oh my dear, oh my dear?
Will you wear blue, Jennie Jenkins?
  No, I won't wear blue,
  For the color's too true.
Chorus

Will you wear yellow, oh my dear, oh my dear?
Will you wear yellow, Jennie Jenkins?
  No, I won't wear yellow,
  For I'd never get a fellow.
Chorus

Will you wear brown, oh my dear, oh my dear?
Will you wear brown, Jennie Jenkins?
  No, I won't wear brown,
  For I'd never get around.
Chorus

Will you wear beige, oh my dear, oh my dear?
Will you wear beige, Jennie Jenkins?
  No, I won't wear beige,
  For it shows my age.
Chorus

Will you wear orange, oh my dear, oh my dear?
Will you wear orange, Jennie Jenkins?
  No, orange I won't wear,
  And it rhymes — so there!
Chorus

What will you wear, oh my dear, oh my dear?
What will you wear, Jennie Jenkins?
  Oh, what do you care
  If I just go bare?
Chorus

Hey Lolly, Lolly

I may be right and I may be wrong,
  Hey lolly, lolly lo.
But I know you're gonna sing this song,
  Hey lolly, lolly lo.
Chorus

I know a girl who's ten feet tall,
  Hey lolly, lolly lo.
Sleeps in the kitchen with her feet in the hall,
  Hey lolly, lolly lo.
Chorus

Everybody sing the chorus,
  Hey lolly, lolly lo.
Either you're against us or you're for us,
  Hey lolly, lolly lo.
Chorus

The purpose of this little song,
  Hey lolly, lolly lo.
Is to make up verses as you go along,
  Hey lolly, lolly lo.
Chorus

Kookaburra

4-part round

Kook - a - bur - ra sits on an old gum tree____

Mer - ry, mer - ry king, of the bush is he____ Laugh kook - a - bur - ra,

laugh kook - a - bur - ra Gay your life must be.

Kookaburra sits on the old gum tree,
Eating all the gum drops he can see.
Stop! Kookaburra stop! Kookaburra,
Leave some there for me.

Dona Nobis Pacem

Give us peace
3-part round

Latin

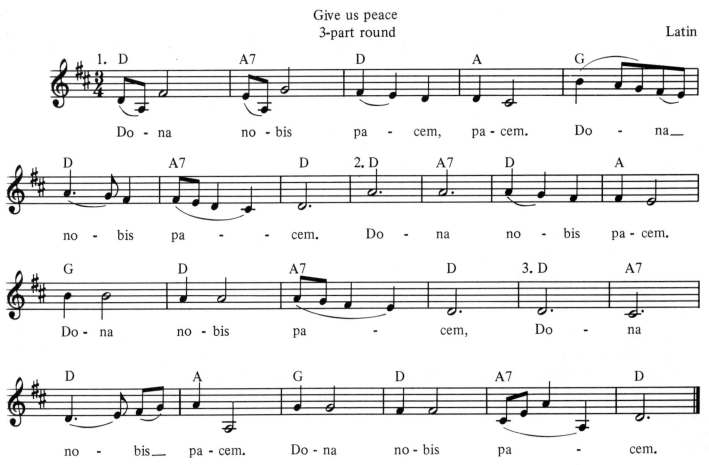

Do - na no - bis pa - cem, pa - cem. Do - na____

no - bis pa - cem. Do - na no - bis pa - cem.

Do - na no - bis pa - cem, Do - na

no - bis____ pa - cem. Do - na no - bis pa - cem.

Who Did Swallow Jonah?

Who did, who did, who did, who did, Who did swal-low Jo - Jo - Jo - nah,

1. Who did, who did, who did, who did, Who did swal - low Jo - Jo - Jo - nah?

2. Who did swal-low Jo - nah, Who did swal-low Jo - nah, Who did swal-low Jo - nah down?

The whale did (4) The whale did ⎤3
  swallow Jo-Jo-Jonah
The whale did swallow Jonah (2)
The whale did swallow Jonah, up.

Shadrack (4) Shadrack, Meshak ⎤3
  Abindigo
Shadrack, Meshak, Abindi (2)
  Shadrack, Meshak, Abindi-go.

Gabriel (4) blow your trum-trum-trum-trum⎤3
Gabriel, blow your trumpet (2)
Gabriel, blow your trumpet loud.

Noah (4) in the ark-ark-arky⎤3
Noah in the arky (2)
Noah in the arky bailed.

David (4) killed Goli li liath⎤4
David killed Goliath (2)
David killed Goliath dead.

Daniel (4) Daniel in the li-li-lion's 3⎤
Daniel in the lion's (2)
Daniel in the lion's deu.

The Streets Of Glory

Gospel Song

Rhythmically

I'm gon-na walk the streets of glo - ry,

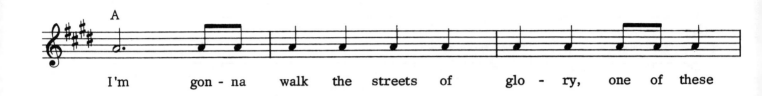

I'm gon-na walk the streets of glo-ry, one of these

days, hal-le-lu-jah, I'm gon-na walk the streets of glo -

ry, Walk the streets of glo-ry one of these days. ____

I'm gonna tell God how you treat me,
I'm gonna tell God how you treat me,
   One of these days, hallelujah.
I'm gonna tell God how you treat me,
Tell God how you treat me, one of these days.

I'm gonna walk and talk with Jesus...

Repeat Verse One

Careless Love

American Folk Song

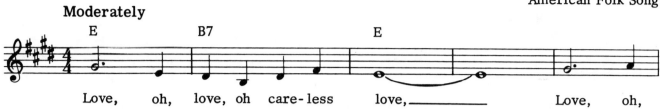

I cried last night and the night before,
I cried last night and the night before,
I cried last night and the night before,
Gonna cry tonight and cry no more.

I love my momma and my poppa too, (*3 times*)
But I'd leave them both to go with you.

When I wore an apron low, (*3 times*)
You'd follow me through rain and snow.

Now I wear my apron high, (*3 times*)
You see my door and pass on by.

How I wish that train would come, (*3 times*)
And take me back where I come from.

Repeat Verse One

Drill, Ye Tarriers, Drill

American Work Song

Now, our new foreman was Jim McCann,
By God, he was a blame mean man.
Last week a premature blast went off,
And a mile in the air went Big Jim Goff,
And drill, ye tarriers, drill.
Chorus

The next time payday come around,
Jim Goff a dollar short was found.
When he asked, "What for?", came this reply,
"You're docked for the time you was up in the sky,"
And drill, ye tarriers, drill.
Chorus

Now the boss was a fine man down to the ground,
And he married a lady six feet round;
She baked good bread and she baked it well,
But she baked it hard as the holes in hell,
And drill, ye tarriers, drill.
Chorus

Skip To My Lou

Lively
Chorus

Children's Folk Song

Skip, skip, skip to my lou, Skip, skip, skip to my lou,

Skip, skip, skip to my lou, Skip to my lou, my dar - ling.

Lost my partner, what'll I do,
Lost my partner, what'll I do,
Lost my partner, what'll I do,
Skip to my lou, my darling.
Chorus

I'll get another one prettier than you, (*3 times*)
Skip to my lou, my darling.
Chorus

Flies in the buttermilk, shoo, fly, shoo, (*3 times*)
Skip to my lou, my darling.
Chorus

Little red wagon painted blue, (*3 times*)
Skip to my lou, my darling.
Chorus

Gone again, skip to my lou, (*3 times*)
Skip to my lou, my darling.
Chorus

The Noble Duke Of York

Oh, the grand old Duke of York,
He had ten thousand men,
They waved their flags to the top of the hill
And they waved them down again. *Chorus*

Oh, the grand old Duke of York,
He had ten thousand men,
They played their pipes to the top of the hill
And they played them down again. *Chorus*

Oh, the grand old Duke of York,
He had ten thousand men,
They fired their guns to the top to the hill
And they fired them down again. *Chorus*

Alouette

French Canadian

A - lou - et - te, gen - tille A - lou - et - te, A - lou - et - te,

Je te plu - me - rai   Je te plu - me - rai 1. la tête,   Je te plu - me - rai 1. la tête.

2. le bec	2. le bec
3. le cou	3. le cou
4. les jambes	4. les jambes
5. les pieds	5. les pieds
6. les pattes	6. les pattes

D.C. al Fine

Et la tête, Et la tête, A - lou-ette, A - lou-ette, Oh _____

*sim. Repeat cumulatively
back to "tête"*

Fillimiooriay

Irish-American Folk Song

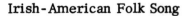

In eighteen hundred and forty-two,
I left the old world for the new,
Bad cess to the luck that brought me through
To work upon the railway.
Chorus

In eighteen hundred and forty-three,
'Twas then I met sweet Biddy McGee,
An elegant wife she's been to me,
While working on the railway.
Chorus

It's "Pat, do this," and "Pat, do that,"
Without a stocking or cravat,
And nothing but an old straw hat,
While working on the railway.
Chorus

In eighteen hundred and forty-six,
They pelted me with stones and sticks,
Oh, I was in a terrible fix,
While working on the railway.
Chorus

In eighteen hundred and forty-seven,
Sweet Biddy McGee, she went to heaven.
If she left one child, she left eleven,
To work upon the railway.
Chorus

82

Father Abraham

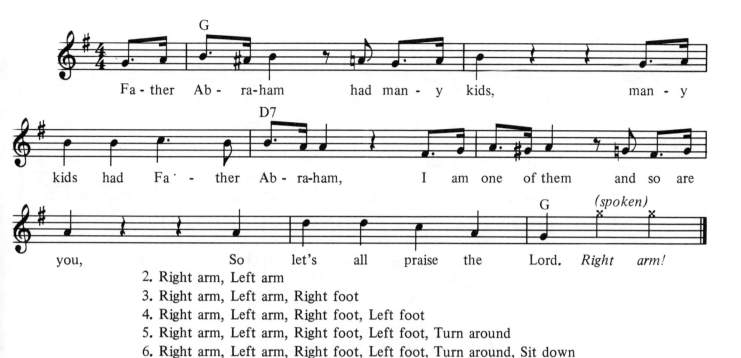

Fa - ther Ab - ra - ham had man - y kids, man - y kids had Fa - ther Ab - ra-ham, I am one of them and so are you, So let's all praise the Lord. *Right arm!* (spoken)

2. Right arm, Left arm
3. Right arm, Left arm, Right foot
4. Right arm, Left arm, Right foot, Left foot
5. Right arm, Left arm, Right foot, Left foot, Turn around
6. Right arm, Left arm, Right foot, Left foot, Turn around, Sit down

Oats, Peas And Barley Grow

Oats, peas, beans and bar - ley grow, oats, peas, beans and bar - ley grow, can you or I or an - y one know, How oats, peas, beans and bar - ley grow.

Wait - ing for a part - ner, wait - ing for a part - ner, o - pen the ring and bring on in, while we all gai - ly dance and sing.

Here's the farmer sowing seed,
Thus he stands and takes his ease.
Stamping his foot and clasping his hands,
He turns around and views his lands.
Tra la la la la la la,
Tra la la la la la la.
Tra la la la la la la la,
Tra la la la la la la la.

Once There Were Three Fishermen

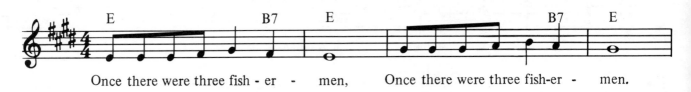

Once there were three fish - er - men, Once there were three fish-er - men.

Fish - er, fish - er, fish - er - men, Fish - er, fish - er, fish - er - men. Once there were three fish - er - men.

The first one's name was Abraham, (2x)
Abra, Abra, ham ham ham, (2x)
The first one's name was Abraham.

continue similarly
The second one's name was Isaac,
Isa Isa ack ack ack

The third one's name was Jacob,
Jakey, Jakey cub cub cub

They all sailed up to Amsterdam,
Amster Amster shh shh shh

The Sidewalks Of New York
Words and Music by
C.B. Lawlor and
J.W. Blake

East side, west side, all a - round the town.____

Tots sang "Ring-a - round Ros-ie," "Lon - don Bridge is fall - ing down."____

Boys and girls to - geth-er,_____ Me and Ma-mie O' - rourke____

Tripped the light__ fan - tas-tic on the side-walks of New York.____

I'm On My Way

Spiritual

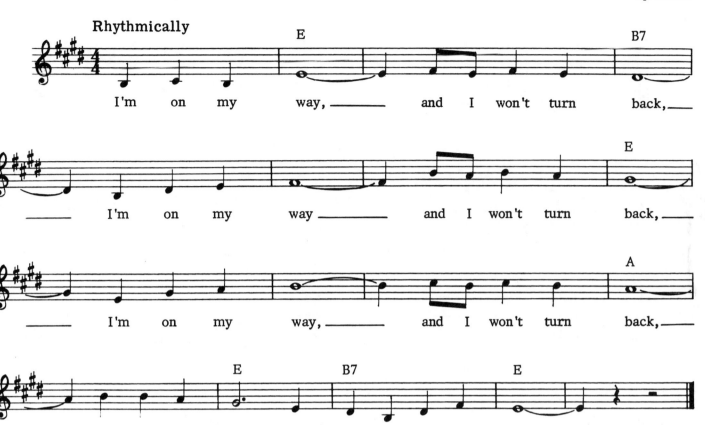

I asked my brother to come with me,
I asked my brother to come with me,
I asked my brother to come with me,
  I'm on my way, great God, I'm on my way.

If he won't come, I'll go alone,
If he won't come, I'll go alone,
If he won't come, I'll go alone,
  I'm on my way, great God, I'm on my way.

I asked my sister to come with me,
I asked my sister to come with me,
I asked my sister to come with me,
  I'm on my way, great God, I'm on my way.

If she won't come, I'll go alone,
If she won't come, I'll go alone,
If she won't come, I'll go alone,
  I'm on my way, great God, I'm on my way.

I asked my boss to let me go,
I asked my boss to let me go,
I asked my boss to let me go,
  I'm on my way, great God, I'm on my way.

If he says no, I'll go anyhow,
If he says no, I'll go anyhow,
If he says no, I'll go anyhow,
  I'm on my way, great God, I'm on my way.

I'm on my way to the Promised Land,
I'm on my way to the Promised Land,
I'm on my way to the Promised Land,
  I'm on my way, great God, I'm on my way.

Repeat Verse One

Old Time Religion

Spiritual

Chorus

Give me that old time re - li - gion, Give me that old time re - li - gion, Give me that old time re - li - gion, It's good e - nough for me, It was good for the He - brew chil - dren, It was good for the He - brew chil - dren, It was good for the he - brew chil - dren, And it's good e - nough for me!

It was good for Paul and Silas,
It was good for Paul and Silas,
It was good for Paul and Silas,
It's good enough for me. *Chorus*

It'll be good when the world's on fire,
It'll be good when the world's on fire,
It'll be good when the world's on fire,
It's good enough for me. *Chorus*

Goin' Down the Road Feelin' Bad

Southern Folk Song

Rhythmically

I'm goin' down the road feel - in' bad, _____ Lord, I'm

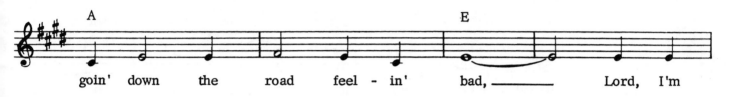

goin' down the road feel - in' bad, _____ Lord, I'm

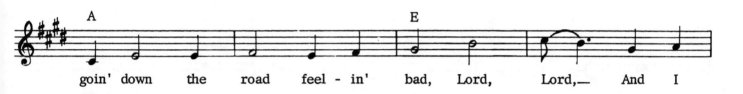

goin' down the road feel - in' bad, Lord, Lord, — And I

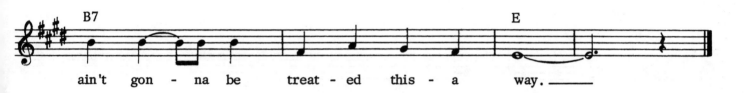

ain't gon - na be treat - ed this - a way. _____

I'm going where the climate suits my clothes (*3 times*)
And I ain't gonna be treated this-a way.

I'm tired of lying in this jail, (*3 times*)
And I ain't gonna be treated this-a way.

I'm going where the water tastes like wine, (*3 times*)
'Cause this prison water tastes like turpentine.

Two dollar shoes hurt my feet, (*3 times*)
And I ain't gonna be treated this-a way.

Ten dollar shoes suit me fine, (*3 times*)
And I ain't gonna be treated this-a way.

I'm going where the chilly winds don't blow (*3 times*)
And I ain't gonna be treated this-a way.

John B.

West Indian Folk Song

Moderate Calypso

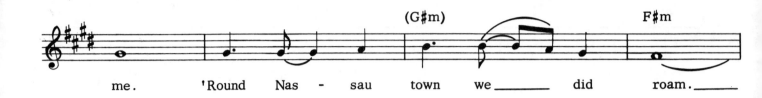

We come on the sloop, John B., My grand - fa - ther and

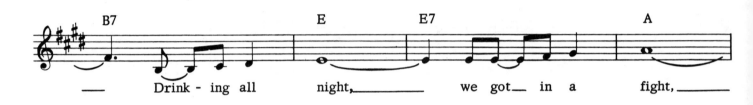

me. 'Round Nas - sau town we did roam.

Drink - ing all night, we got in a fight,

I feel so break up, I want to go home.

Chorus: So hoist up the John B. sails,
See how the mainsail sets,
Send for the captain ashore, let me go home.
Let me go home, let me go home,
I feel so break up,
I want to go home.

The first mate, oh, he got drunk,
Broke up the people's trunk,
Constable had to come and take him away.
Sheriff Johnstone please leave me alone,
I feel so break-up, I want to go home.
Chorus

The poor cook, oh, he got fits,
Ate up all of the grits.
Then he took and threw away all of the corn.
Sheriff Johnstone please leave me alone,
This is the worst trip I ever been on.
Chorus

Camptown Races

By Stephen Foster

The long-tail filly and the big black hoss,
  Doo-dah, doo-dah,
They fly the track and they both cut across,
  Oh, doo-day day.
The blind hoss sticken in a big mud hole,
  Doo-dah, doo-dah,
Can't touch bottom with a ten-foot pole,
  Oh, doo-day day.
Chorus

Old muley cow come onto the track,
  Doo-dah, doo-dah,
The bobtail fling her over his back,
  Oh, doo-day day.
Then fly along like a railroad car,
  Doo-dah, doo-dah,
Running a race with a shooting star,
  Oh, doo-day day.
Chorus

See them flying on a ten-mile heat,
  Doo-dah, doo-dah,
'Round the race track, then repeat,
  Oh, doo-day day.
I win my money on the bobtail nag,
  Doo-dah, doo-dah,
I keep my money in an old towbag,
  Oh, doo-day day.
Chorus

Hail! Hail! The Gang's All Here

Lively

G
Hail! hail,— the gang's all here, what the heck do we care, what the heck do we care,

G   D7   G
Hail, hail,— the gang's all here, what the heck do we care now?—

Hey Ho, Nobody's Home

3-part round

Hey ho, no-bod-y's home, No meat, nor drink, nor mon-ey have I none,

Still I will be mer - ry,— Hey ho, no-bod-y's home, No meat, nor drink, nor mon-ey have I none,

Still I will be mer - ry — Hey ho, no-bod-y's home.—

Hi! Cheerily Ho

3-part round

Hi! Cheer - i - ly, ho, mer - ri - ly, ho,

Sail - ors are we, sons of the sea, sing - ing with

glee. Hi, ho, hi, ho!

99 Bottles On The Wall

Lively

Nine - ty-nine bot-tles of slime* on the wall, Nine - ty nine bot-tles of slime,___ and

one fell down and broke its crown, Nine - ty-eight bot-tles of slime on the wall.

*Bottles of other liquids may be used in this song!

2. 98 Bottles, etc.
3. 97 Bottles, etc.
4. 96 Bottles, etc.

John Jacob Jingleheimer Schmidt

John   Ja - cob   Jin - gle - heim-er Schmidt,   His   name is my   name

too!_____   when - ev - er   we go out,   all the   peo - ple yell and shout,

"John   Ja - cob Jin - gle - heim - er   Schmidt, Da - Da - Da - Da - Da - Da - Da."

2. Here comes the Puppy dog patrol,
   Your dog and my dog too!
   Whenever we go out we can hear the boy scouts shout,
   "Here comes the puppy dog patrol,
   Bow - wow - wow - wow - wow - wow - wow

I Love The Mountains

Round

I love the moun-tains, I love the roll-ing hills, I love the flow-ers,

I love the daf-fo-dils, I love the fire-side When all the lights are low,

Boom - dee - ah - da, boom - dee - ah - da, Boom - dee - ah - da, boom - dee - ah - da,

Boom - dee - ah - da, boom - dee - ah - da, Boom - dee - ah - da, boom - dee - ah - da,

I've Been Working On The Railroad

Chords Used In This Book

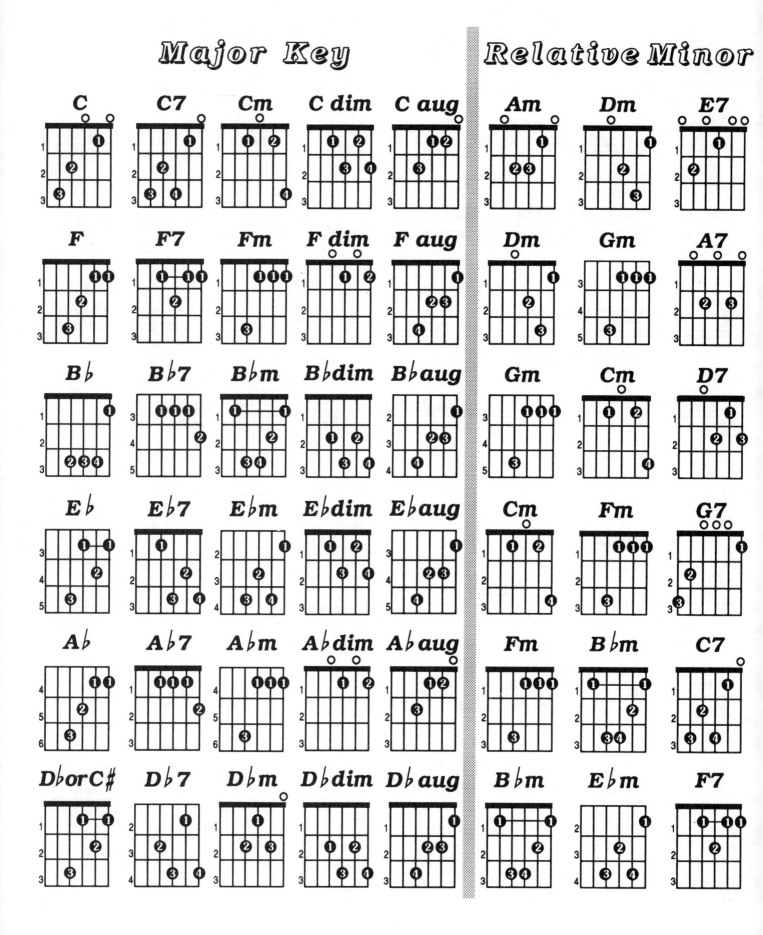

Major Key

Relative Minor

G♭ or F♯ **G♭7** **G♭m** **G♭dim** **G♭aug** | **E♭m** **A♭m** **B♭7**

      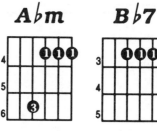

B **B7** **Bm** **B dim** **B aug** | **G♯m** **C♯m** **D♯7**

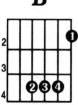 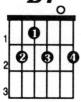 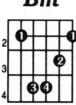   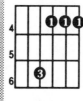  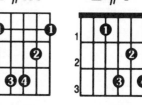

E **E7** **Em** **E dim** **E aug** | **C♯m** **F♯m** **G♯7**

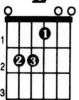   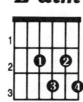 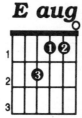 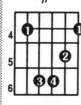 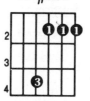 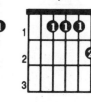

A **A7** **Am** **A dim** **A aug** | **F♯m** **Bm** **C♯7**

 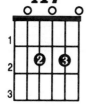  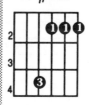 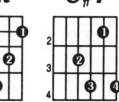

D **D7** **Dm** **D dim** **D aug** | **Bm** **Em** **F♯7**

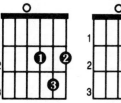 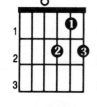 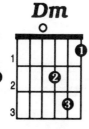 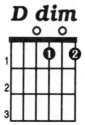 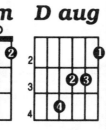 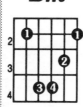 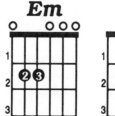

G **G7** **Gm** **G dim** **G aug** | **Em** **Am** **B7**

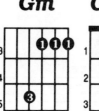 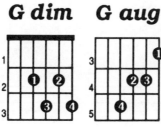  

95